Earlyarts Pocket Guides

Cultural Entitlement in a Nutshell

Revised 2012 Version

Almost everything you need to know about designing and delivering a Cultural Offer

by Ruth Churchill Dower

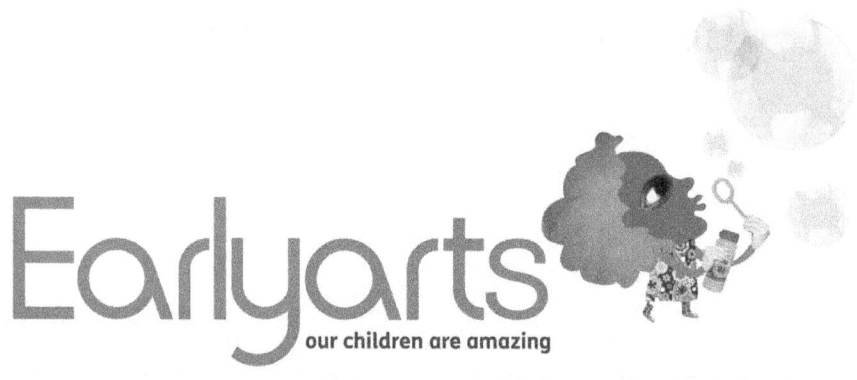

our children are amazing

Cultural Entitlement in a Nutshell

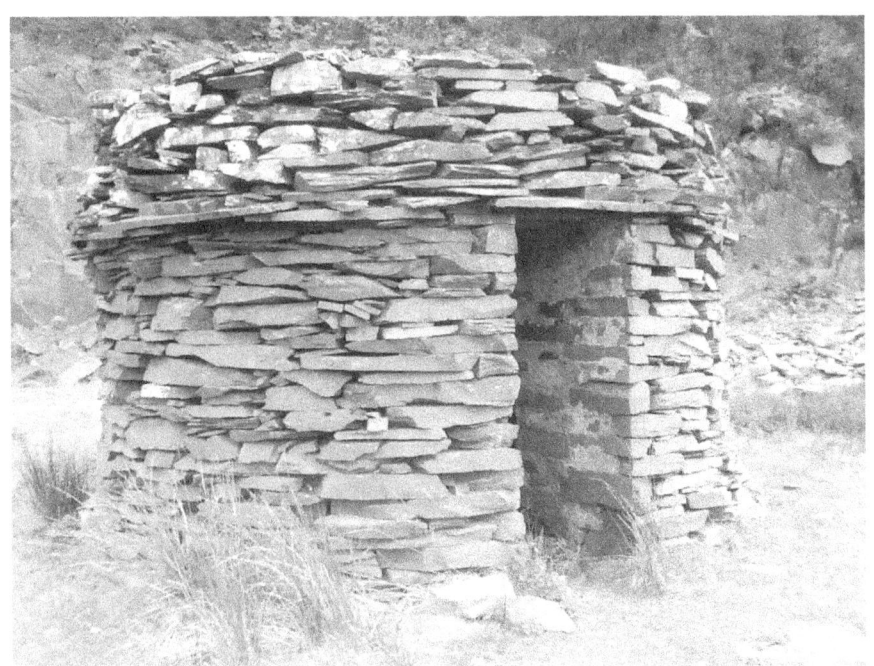

Bus Stop Quarry, Llanberis. Image by Ruth Churchill Dower

Introduction

Earlyarts' series of Pocket Guides aims to help professionals in the arts, cultural, education and children's services sectors find their way through the quagmire of buzz words, policies and initiatives that are sometimes in danger of stagnating us all.

What really matters to us is practice – grass roots, hard hitting, thought provoking, people based, bare-bones, sleeves-rolled-up practice. Let's face it, that's what makes the real difference to people's lives. We're constantly inspired and invigorated by those who are passionate enough to join up the dots and make high quality stuff happen. Fantastic. But we also know about practice that, frankly, isn't really raising the quality of our children's lives for a whole variety of reasons that we'd like to influence.

Whether you're a policy maker or practitioner, if you're feeling overwhelmed, stuck, confused, or just downright bored with it all, we very much hope this little guide will help you to feel slightly clearer, challenged and inspired to make a difference. The tools and opportunities are out there. It's up to us to make it happen.

An enormous debt of gratitude goes to the thinkers and doers who have gone before and whose work, thoughts and ideas have inspired the content of this guide. Not everything out there is represented in here (please tell us if something crucial is missing, as we can update the online publication). Not everything will be relevant – you can pick and choose to suit your context. We have tried to capture the main issues, ideas and initiatives, bringing them together into one place to make it easier for busy people to use.

Thanks go to the Cultural Strategy Team at Manchester City Council whose commission provided some of the research that led to this Guide being published.

All proceeds from this Pocket Guide go to Earlyarts, the award winning national network for professionals working creatively with young children and families – providing the best possible start in life.

Contents

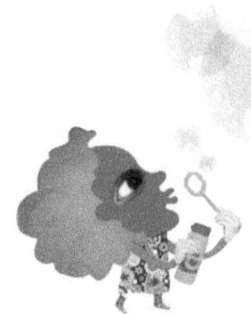

Pocket Guide No. 1
Cultural Entitlement in a Nutshell

What's the Big Idea?

Cultural Entitlement is one of those elastic phrases that can be stretched to cover a number of agendas. However, at its heart is a fundamental belief in the **rights of all children and young people** to access, create, participate in and benefit from cultural opportunities. This is currently not the case and recent government initiatives are intended to support professionals in developing these opportunities in a genuinely rich and meaningful way. For our part, the cultural and education or children's services sectors must take responsibility to ensure that their **cultural provision (or 'offer') meets children's and young people's needs** by being interesting, relevant, responsive and valuable to them, underpinning their various social and cultural identities, building a sense of belonging and empowerment, and helping them to find their 'fit' within the bigger picture.

In order to recognise and support the complexity of our children and young people's identities, we need to investigate, listen, understand, respect and celebrate who our children are now – not just focus on preparing them for the future. The potential **power of our provision to transform children's lives** might be obvious to us, but with the mass of neurological changes going on inside children and young people's brains[1], the increasing economic, social and environmental pressures on many families, and the rise in choice of opportunity, we need to make it as easy as possible for them to want to be involved. Therefore the

---

[1] see **Young Brains**, DfES Research Report no. 444 (2003). Young Brains report

manifestation of a cultural entitlement should be **personalised** to the individual child or young person.

In a policy-driven culture, the biggest challenge is to resist using the jigsaw of cross-referenced policy objectives as the starting point for defining the place of culture in young people's lives. A true entitlement model keeps the child at the heart rather than trying to find the 'best fit'. The child's needs, aspirations, ideas and potential should be the **starting points for all provision** (i.e. cultural, social and health care, community, transport, employment, and so on) in ways which add value to the child's life and that of their families and peers. Often, multiple policy objectives are more than fulfilled anyway through a child-oriented approach, leading to more joined up, holistic and meaningful provision for the target group.

There has been much debate as to the definitions of culture, in relation to people's entitlement. Many consider it part of a **citizenship agenda**, supporting children's social and emotional development, as well as developing the key attributes necessary to achieve a quality of life. Others focus on the exploration of **diversity amongst many different cultures** and cultural identities, enabling us to develop a broader understanding of who we are, our place in the world, and issues of belonging. Some revolve around the idea of **access to engage with culture**, usually a cultural product or experience, often designed to enrich life or lead to more positive human qualities. Others still refer to the term as meaning the opportunity to raise awareness, interpretation and **understanding of our cultural heritage**, in terms of historical identities, events or objects across the globe. There is also the view that cultural entitlement is largely about **audience development** in terms of preparing future consumers of culture, but not necessarily participating in it.

What is generally agreed is that our provision, or **cultural offer**, should aim to harness **effective cultural experiences**, particularly for those who would not normally access cultural opportunities for themselves. That means not just a richness and diversity of provision, but also a strong infrastructure that offers schools, settings and other organisations the chance to make and sustain their connections with good quality provision. There is nothing wrong with professionals leading on the design of great new cultural opportunities and products for children, as long as every planner or deliverer of the cultural offer starts by consulting on, and understanding what 'success' looks like from the perspective of their specific age group or target audience. It is up to us as adults, professionals, or volunteers working with children and young people, to **help them to achieve their cultural entitlement**.

Find Your Talent (a government initiative to help achieve a strong 'Cultural Offer' everywhere) was the **first public policy for culture that required an obligation to achieve universal provision**, i.e. a cultural opportunity for every single child in the country – it was predicated on access for all. It put **culture on a similar footing to health and education**, as much a part of free state provision, but without a statutory infrastructure, or any way of fully measuring children's engagement with culture, or its impact on their lives. The main strategic challenges therefore were around how Cultural Offer teams built the infrastructure, connected the many agencies involved, adequately supported the capacity of providers, measured its immediate and potential impact, and still kept the programme focussed on the child or young person.

Over the last decade, UK education policy has moved towards a more holistic view of the child that takes account of their wider world, including their family context, health and social care needs as well as their educational development. This integrated approach policy, exemplified by **Every Child Matters** and the **Children's (and Young People's) Plan**, was reflected in the joining up of children's services at national and local authority levels. Every Child Matters is arranged around five themes, leading to what are considered the most important outcomes for all children in today's contexts: Be healthy; Stay safe; Enjoy and achieve; Make a positive contribution; Achieve economic well-being. **Cultural provision** has a role to play in all five, but probably **makes the strongest contribution to achieving the first, third and fourth outcomes**.

National initiatives including Living Places, Extended Schools, Learning outside the Classroom, Earlyarts, Creative Partnerships, and many others all shared **a universal agreement as to the fundamental benefits of sports, play, arts and culture** to individual strength, community cohesion and regeneration. The vision for the healthy and balanced development (physical, social and emotional) of children and young people is threaded through most policies, driven by the government's core objectives of increasing economic productivity, expanding economic and employment opportunities, and eradicating child poverty and material deprivation by 2020.

The emphasis for achieving this has been very much on extending the range of services offered by cultural and education or children's services providers to make sure children (from birth), young people and families have the support and opportunities they need to thrive. The government is also keenly aware of the skills and attitudes needed for industry in the future, and intends to help the various sectors involved prepare our students to be successful in the workforce. Again, cultural and creative practices have a major role to play in helping young people develop independence, critical thinking and problem solving skills, flexible approaches to working and **resilience to cope with the changing industrial, technological and social environments**.

The strategies for achieving these outcomes through our cultural provision are reflected fairly coherently through the many different policies championed by government departments, and broadly focus around the following key themes: **infrastructure development** both within and across our sectors towards more integrated services at the point of delivery; **connectivity and transfer of knowledge** and convergence of policy, practice, research and pedagogy; **workforce development** through training, CPD and enriched leadership; **monitoring and assessment** processes that significantly enhance reflective practice and provide a rigorous evidence base showing the positive impacts of culture and creativity on learning and development; **strategic planning and delivery of cultural programmes** that are child / young person / family oriented, and help to enhance self-confidence, improve relationships, raise aspirations and produce better attitudes to learning.

If our cultural and learning provision is geared towards enhancing the quality of lives for children, young people, and their families, then we need to focus on understanding who and what our children want to be, both now and in the future. This means their knowledge and understanding, attitudes and attributes, competences and skills, connections and opportunities.

Next we need to look at what our position is now, what is helping and what is stopping our children and young people achieve these goals, and what our own organisations can do to help this process.

In reality it will require a shift in attitudes as well as infrastructure to enable our professionals across the sectors to work purposefully together. Some Local Authorities have established cross-agency agreements that will go some way towards setting out the requirements for different delivery routes to respond effectively to local need, but if the aim of policy makers is to make a reality of their commitment to cultural entitlement, then the capacity of the whole sector needs to be strengthened or rebuilt to meet this challenge. A clear advocacy role exists for the cultural providers to articulate how opportunities for culture and creativity in their local communities should be progressed.

However, significant change may arise only if the benefits of creative approaches to life and access to cultural provision are embedded within the resources, planning, training, delivery and assessment of all cultural provision. In short, it needs providers to be truly committed to helping all communities achieve their cultural entitlement.

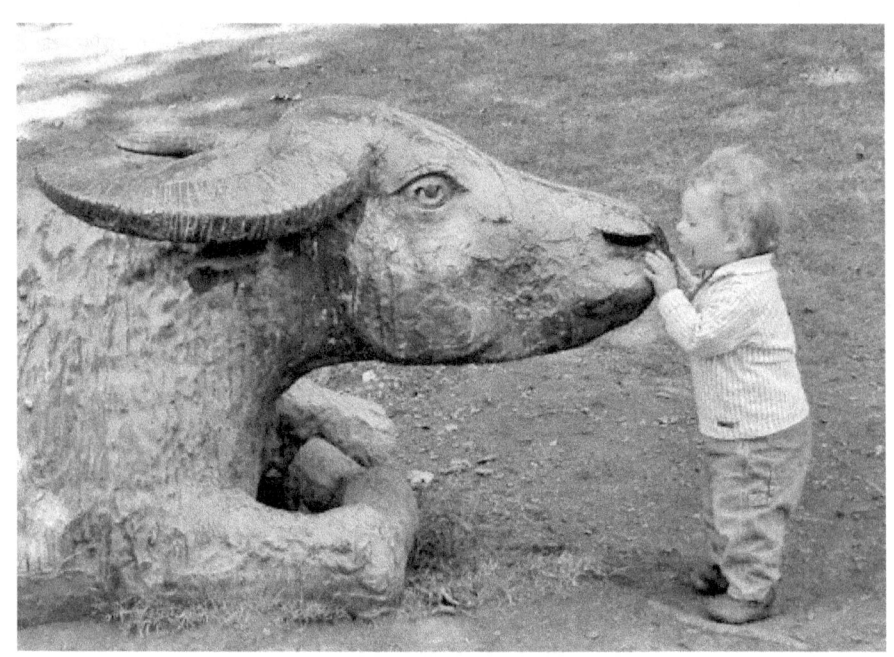

Yorkshire Sculpture Park. Image by Ruth Churchill Dower

20 Big Questions for designing a Cultural Offer that helps everybody achieve their entitlement

Strategy and Programming:

- How do we stay focussed on children and young people, and base our activity on clear expectations and outcomes, without becoming tokenistic?

- How do we build a culture of compassion and responsibility for our youngest individuals across several professional sectors, many of whom are not primarily engaged with young people?

- How can we remove the barriers to embedding an entitlement to culture within every practice of every partner involved? Or, how do we establish a place for culture in all cross-sector agreements in relation to children's services, workforce development, social cohesion, community sustainability, play, transport and regeneration?

- How do we reduce the current fragmentation in addressing the needs of children, and how do we enable multiple policy objectives to be fulfilled at the same time to reduce overload and inefficiency?

- What is it that creates a compelling, inspiring, and possibly life changing cultural experience? How can our organisation contribute to delivering that?

- How do we really help children and young people tell their own stories, to express their ideas and feelings, to find out who they are, and to have adults understand and take them seriously?

- Can our cultural offer support progression routes for families into communities, for young people into employment, and for communities into regeneration?

- Can we use existing models to shape an infrastructure that fulfils our key objectives for participation, cross-agency collaboration, recognising achievement, or measuring quality, such as *Hear by Right*, *Arts Awards*, *Inspiring Learning for All*, and so on?

Inclusion:

- How do we genuinely address inequality and increase participation for those who don't normally have access, rather than extending provision for those who already know what they want and how to get it?

- How do we use the cultural offer to ensure the voice of children and young people is truly represented and influencing provision, so that it can directly respond to their needs and supports their aspirations?

- How can we offer children and young people a sense of autonomy, responsibility for, and control over their cultural involvement?

- Can we change our own cultures to ensure that learning is at the heart, i.e. that it is properly represented at senior management and board level; that the expertise of learning teams is valued and developed; and that the needs of children, families, carers and other learners from the wider community are identified and addressed.

Connectivity of Infrastructure and Capacity Building:

- How can the cultural offer programme add value to

the existing infrastructure, specifically considering the need for better connectivity and information sharing, professional development and leadership development, business growth and sustainability, resource development and legacy support, united messages and marketing approaches, and cross-agency working?

- What brokerage processes can we use to connect the different pillars of support in children's and young people's lives (e.g. a map of opportunity), in order that each provider is aware of opportunities to engage with other complementary providers?

- Can our cultural venues be better shared by local communities for learning, family support, employment, social and health care as well as cultural activities, and can this engender a longer term loyalty amongst a broader range of users?

- What do we want our cultural, social and educational venues or environments to look like in ten years time – can the Cultural Offer journey help to take them there?

Monitoring and Measuring:

- What indicators will tell us how successful the programme has been and what messages do we want to champion, e.g. increased engagement with previous non-attenders; identified benefits of culture on the development of broader competencies and whether those benefits are greater if engagement is sustained; increased long term partnerships between educational, social and cultural providers; ways to measure the impacts of creative processes that are not product oriented?

- Are there existing models that can be used or adapted to properly measure the impact of the programme, such as the Generic Learning Outcomes in _Inspiring Learning for All_, the _School Improvement Planning Framework_ originally developed by the TDA for Schools?

- How do we gather information to reflect on the success and the challenges of the programme, e.g. can old and new technology be harnessed for the purposes of research, consultation, documentation, planning and review, capturing people's own stories, advocacy and promotion? Can social media help connect young people with cultural providers, e.g. by offering opportunities for self generated user assessments of quality; suitability; usefulness and growing a community of online Cultural Champions, or by engaging them in longer term learning about their cultural identities and experiences using journals or blogs?

- Can the cultural offer provide a platform to commission, collate and interpret more robust research linked in to national strategies e.g. the impacts of the programme on specific objectives such as regeneration, or the characteristics of sustainable collaborative processes? Can research be done in such a way as to create shared, effective models for identifying, evaluating and disseminating best practice in enabling children, families and young people to achieve their cultural entitlement?

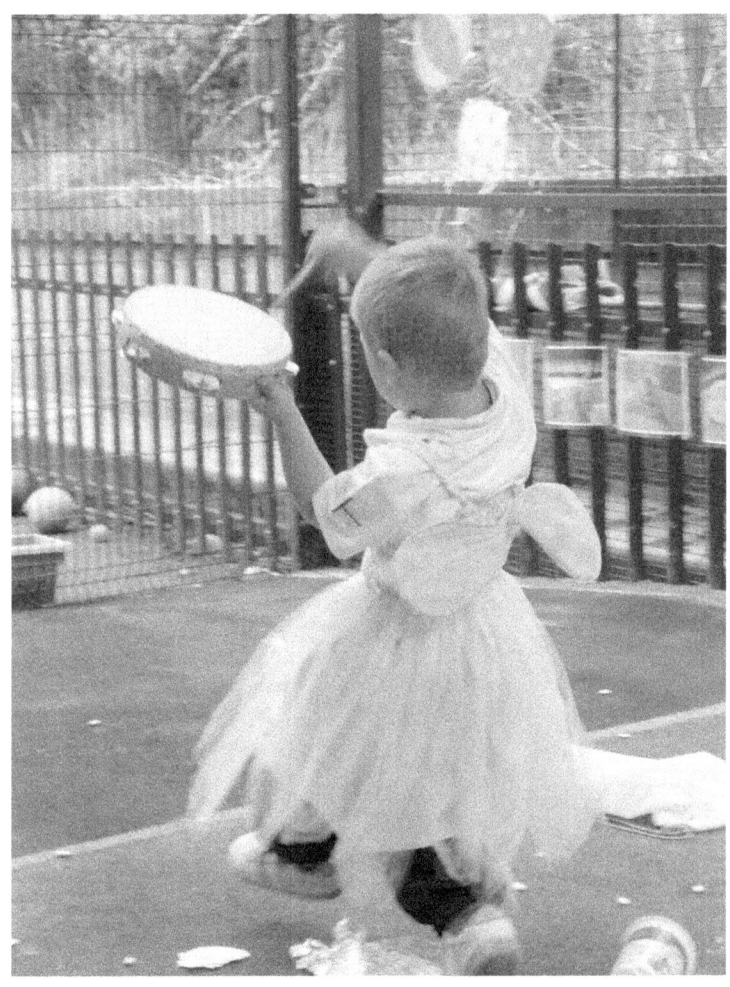

Life at a Manchester Children's Centre. Image by Ruth Churchill Dower

Cultural Entitlement Policy and Pedagogy Road Map

- **UN Convention on the Rights of the Child (1989)** enshrines the duty of governments to ensure that children have a right to express their views, have them taken account of (Article 12), to engage in play appropriate to the age of the child and to participate freely in cultural life and the arts (Article 31).

- **National Advisory Committee for Creative and Cultural Education (NACCCE) report (1999)** 'All Our Futures' was a ground breaking report in its time and has influenced much policy development in creative and cultural learning. It emphasised the importance of **developing the creative capacities of young people** and the power of culture to help them engage positively with the growing complexity and diversity of social values and ways of life, and to **access their cultural entitlement.** The report called for a recognition of creativity within national priorities; embedding creative processes into the curriculum; new approaches to teaching and learning; cultural education as a route to raising standards; the need for assessment to support rather than inhibit creativity; and the need to establish better systems of funding, training and quality assurance of the impact and effectiveness of partnerships.

- **Creative Partnerships (2002)** was the Government's flagship creative learning programme, designed to develop the creativity and enterprise of young people, raising their aspirations and achievements. They nurtured innovative, long-term partnerships between schools and creative practitioners to challenge how they work, their approaches to culture, creativity and partnership working. They also aimed to foster the skills, capacity and sustainability of the creative industries, and other partners, in ways that could **broaden and deepen their cultural and creative offer to young people** and inspire learning.

- DfES Primary National Strategy: Excellence and Enjoyment **(2003)** The aim - for every primary school to combine excellence in teaching with enjoyment of learning. Whilst the focus was still on raising standards (particularly in Literacy and Numeracy), this strategy gave schools the autonomy to be much more **flexible, creative and innovative in their approach to the curriculum content and teaching and learning processes**, with the emphasis on creativity and cross-curricular links. This was the first strategy to introduce individual Assessments for Learning enabling teachers to respond better and **tailor learning to meet children's individual needs**, which led to the personalisation agenda. It also provided the bedrock for the Extended Schools agenda, with its emphasis on external partnerships with parents and local communities. Other aims were to tackle leadership, professional development and workforce reform.

- OfSTED Expecting the Unexpected: Developing creativity in primary and secondary schools **(2003)** identified characteristics of successful creative teaching and learning including: teachers having an understanding and experience of creativity; providing the opportunity by **promoting enquiry based learning environments**; good subject knowledge; good relationships with children; reflective assessment processes in order to learn from developments; organisation of a **creative curriculum**; access to quality resources;

links with external cultural and creative programmes such as Creative Partnerships; influential teachers and **visionary leadership for advocacy in creativity**.

- **HM Government Every Child Matters: Change for Children (2004)** set out the Government's strategy to implement the key tenets of the Children Act (2004) to integrate all children's services, and to place the wishes and needs of children's services, parents and learners centre-stage, the main aim being to **improve children's life chances** and their parents' access to work and training. It was founded on five key outcomes: being healthy; staying safe; enjoying and achieving; making a positive contribution; and achieving economic well-being. Sports, Play and **Cultural sectors played a central role** in helping to deliver these five outcomes, particularly in supporting a child's entitlement to **celebrate their own, and others', cultural identities**, encourage their **individual expression**, and to do so within an environment of security, respect and belonging.

- **Paul Roberts' report on Nurturing Creativity in Young People (2006)** A government-commissioned review of creativity in schools with a view to setting out future policy in this area. The report identified the wide range but patchy coverage of creative and cultural provision, recommending a framework for brokering a more cohesive 'offer'. The progression within this framework **starting with the Early Years**, was **embedded** in mainstream education and beyond, developed a **personalised** approach that was inclusive of, and **responsive to, the voices** of children and young people and led to pathways into the Creative Industries.

- <u>Government response to the Paul Roberts' Report</u> **(2006)** reinforced that creativity is not limited to the arts but should be embedded across the whole curriculum, in partnerships with the cultural sector. It discussed how creativity can help to **raise standards**, should produce outcomes of real value, enable children to make a valuable contribution to society, and help them **achieve more personalised learning** (i.e. removing the barriers to achieving their learning goals). This was the first government publication to make **explicit links between creativity and the five outcomes** in Every Child Matters. It committed to delivering the eight Key Actions set out in the Roberts framework to better harness arts, culture and new technology towards increased engagement, motivation, and skills in young people. It acknowledged the need for DCSF and DCMS to work more closely together, and established the joint Advisory Board for Creative and Cultural Education to construct a **more coherent creativity and culture offer** that builds strong connections between existing work and the emerging policy contexts.

- <u>DCMS Time for Play: Encouraging greater play opportunities for children and young people</u> **(2006)** affirms that access to play addresses wider programmes for health, regeneration, childcare, extended schools and youth offending, and provides a powerful platform for **reducing inequalities** and **helping children to reach their potential**. Play is of fundamental importance for children and young people's health, well-being and learning, providing enriching experiences that can help develop their emotional and social skills, ability to learn about risks, use their own initiative, and deal with conflict resulting in an improved impact on mental health. The **arts and cultural sectors provide a range of enhanced play opportunities,** experimenting with textures, colours, sounds, rhythm, movement, character building and mark or object making to explore the world and extend their imagination through play. Many arts and cultural organisations work with families, children and young people and are increasingly involving them in the design and development of their services to ensure they are creative and dynamic, particularly in relation to exploratory, open-ended spaces to play using natural materials.

- The Leitch Review of Skills: Prosperity for all in the Global Economy – World Class Skills **(2006).** The Leitch report aimed to identify the UK's optimal skills mix for 2020 to maximise economic growth, productivity and social justice, and set out the balance of responsibility for achieving that skills profile. It shows that the UK must almost double achievements at all levels of skills in order to commit to becoming a world leader in skills by 2020. The implications from this for the cultural sector were fed into the Creative Britain report, which addressed the need for higher education to do more to meet the needs of business, **creative and cultural work placements, to have a greater emphasis on business and entrepreneurial skills,** and to establish wide ranging apprenticeship schemes in the cultural and creative industries. A key pillar of Lord Leitch's vision was that the number of apprenticeships in the UK should be boosted to 500,000 by 2020 (400,000 in England).

- DCSF The Children's Plan: Building Brighter Futures **(2007) and** Guidance on the Children and Young

People's Plan (2009) built on the reforms introduced by Every Child Matters, particularly its holistic approach to childhood and children's outcomes, addressing the well-being of 0-19 year olds, and leading to sustainable communities. It came with an investment of £1.3 billion over three years in a framework to help tackle barriers to learning, improve health, break intergenerational cycles of disadvantage, and allow local authorities to focus on the issues that were most significant for their particular communities. This challenged local authorities to find out about their communities by involving children, families and practitioners in **identifying needs, aspirations and solutions using a participatory approach**. The Children's Plan confirmed that '*Participation in cultural activity is enriching and contributes to the Every Child Matters outcomes*.' The delivery of CYPP was firmly rooted in Local Area Agreements and relied on **cross-agency partnerships, including with culture and education**, for its successful implementation.

- **HM Government Extended Schools initiative (2007)** Based on the evidence that children's experiences greatly influence their outcomes and life chances in later life, this initiative invested £840 million to support the **community cohesion, personalised and informal learning agendas** (i.e. beyond the classroom or early years setting), and to lift families out of poverty cycles. This included an integrated approach of opening up schools for use by local communities, supporting children's learning through opportunities in the wider community, provision for family learning, and offering a 'wraparound' system of dusk to dawn 'educare' to support working parents. It aimed to significantly increase opportunities for **young people to be creative in more informal learning environments** *'where risk taking and imaginative responses can be encouraged'* (emphasis on the cultural sector), as well as calling on **schools to offer extra creative activities** to pupils, including theatre, music, dance, media and visual arts activities.

- <u>DCSF Aiming High for Young People: a ten year strategy for positive activities</u> **(2007)** recognised the impacts of culture, society and skills on young people growing into adulthood and aimed to transform facilities and support services in order that they could take part in enjoyable and purposeful activities, develop new skills and raise their aspirations. It emphasised the evidence that **participation in creative arts and other cultural activities can have a significant impact on young people's outcomes in later life**, in terms of changing attitudes to learning, building resilience, confidence, emotional intelligence, improving behaviour, stimulating initiative, team work, enterprise and creative thinking.

- <u>House of Commons Select Committee report into Creative Partnerships and the Curriculum</u> **(2007)** recognised the importance of creativity in the curriculum as a means of supporting children and young people's **personal development and achievement**; saw creativity as a holistic process rather than the preserve of the arts, understood the need to **embed this within whole school cultures** as opposed to adding burdens through bolt-on initiatives, and highlighted the role of arts and cultural organisations in introducing children to their creative potential. The report also criticised DCSF for regarding creativity as peripheral to their core responsibilities, and for not making more obvious the **opportunities to collaborate with the arts and cultural sectors** in fulfilling Every Child Matters.

- <u>Find Your Talent</u> **(2008)** committed £25 million to allow all school children five hours of high quality culture a week, to complement the further £110 million invested in the **Creative Partnerships** programme (both managed by a new organisation <u>Creativity, Culture and Education</u>). Recognising that the first chance many young people get to develop their creativity comes through engagement with culture, FYT aimed to achieve a **minimum entitlement to a rounded artistic and cultural experience** for every young person. The programme involved lessons about culture – helping young people develop as critical spectators, participants and creators in the cultural world, and learning through culture – using engagement with the arts and other activities to boost creativity, attainment and personal development

- <u>Creative Britain – New Talents for the New Economy</u> **(2006-8)** Designed to support the innovation, growth and productivity of the cultural and creative Industries, it identified education and skills as one of the main drivers to the productivity and growth of the creative economy. The report aimed to **improve the quality of life for all starting in schools, with a new commitment to culture in children's education.** It linked education and the world of work, and it looks to the future with further support for progression routes into creative businesses.

- <u>DCSF Early Years Foundation Stage</u> **(2008)** is a holistic framework for care and learning, focusing on the distinct needs of children from birth to five. Creativity and play are strongly embedded in the EYFS with

Creative Development being one of six areas of learning and development. It promotes the role of **creative processes to help children to make connections** between one area of learning and another and so extend their understanding. It recognises that through creative play children can explore, develop and use their curiosity and imagination to help them make sense of the world and themselves within it. It promotes **links between settings and cultural organisations** to help children practice skills, build up ideas and concepts, think creatively and imaginatively and communicate with others as they investigate and solve problems.

- QCA New Secondary Curriculum: a curriculum for the future (2008) promoted the use of creative processes to enhance learners' broader competences, give them more choice and control over their learning, and raise standards. It emphasised that schools should give young people the **opportunity to learn in arts and cultural organisations and through collaborative partnerships with a range of professionals** on the school site and in workplaces. Leaders were encouraged to build creativity into the school day in a way that reflected the specific needs and interests of their learners, and explore links between subjects and wider aspects of learning. **Creativity and critical thinking were identified as cross-curriculum dimensions**, providing a focus for work within and between subjects and across the curriculum.

- **The Cultural Heritage Blueprint (2009)** set out the six key challenges for workforce development in museums, galleries, built heritage and archaeology, to support training and entry into the sector, sustainable growth and **a renewed focus on people rather than buildings or objects**. It recommends: better entry routes; a more diverse workforce; improved leadership & management; a culture of learning and professional development; staff business and entrepreneurial skills; at risk specialist skills, such as conservation.

- **Get It: The Power of Cultural Learning** (2009) calls for cultural learning to be given a higher priority in government policy, and for schools and cultural organisations to embed cultural learning into the core curriculum, at senior management and board levels. The report, commissioned by the national arts, culture and education bodies, aims to underpin existing national initiatives and reinforce the shared belief that cultural learning has the potential to transform people's lives.

However, it states that realising this potential will require changing the way in which cultural learning is valued and practised in schools and other learning organisations, and to make more explicit ways of working together successfully to develop consistently high-quality cultural learning experiences.

- **National Curriculum Review (2011)** An expert panel reporting on the review suggested that the current curriculum framework narrows too early in a child's education, and that the arts should newly become part of every school's basic curriculum at Key Stage 4. The arts, at Key Stage 4, would combine art and music but also other aspects of the arts (e.g. dance and drama). The expert panel found that **good arts and music education benefits individuals, communities and the nation as a whole**: improving pupil engagement, cognitive development and achievement, including in mathematics and reading. The panel suggested that consideration needs to be given to the **importance of creative subjects to the economic health of the nation.** In other words, the arts subjects in the curriculum have the potential to meet aims and purposes across the economic, cultural, social and personal domains. The report says that provision should be made for pupils to appreciate the national cultures, traditions and values of England and the other nations within the UK, and provide opportunities for the acquisition of knowledge and appreciation in the arts.

The **National Curriculum Review Suite of Documents** sets out the evidence gathered to date by the National Curriculum review. This suite comprises: the report of the review's Expert Panel-; a summary of the evidence gathered about curricula for English, mathematics and science in high-performing jurisdictions; a research report looking at subject breadth in the curricula used in other education jurisdictions; a summary report of the responses to the review's call for evidence.

- **Revised Framework for the Early Years Foundation Stage (2012)** sets the standards that all early years providers must meet to ensure that children learn and develop well and are kept healthy and safe. It promotes teaching and learning to ensure children gain the broad range of knowledge and skills that provide the right foundation for good future progress through school and life. It bases the learning outcomes on three prime areas and four specific areas of learning, underpinned by four clear values for a unique child, positive relationships, an enabling environment and learning and development. One of the specific areas if Expressive Arts and Design, with a clear opportunity for partnerships with the cultural sector, and increased bridging of creative and cultural experiences for families.

- **The Henley Review of Cultural Education** (2012) is an independent review on Cultural Education in England by Darren Henley for the Department of Culture, Media and Sport, and the Department for Education. The review sets firm foundations for the first Cultural Education Plan for the country, acknowledging the important role of the arts and cultural sector in enhancing children's learning and development. It advocates **local cultural partnerships that will enable cultural engagement and excellence to flourish** throughout all walks of life. Joined up cultural education programmes involving the resources of the cultural sector in the development of teaching and learning strategies makes good sense,

raising the confidence and competence of teachers to scaffold children's all-round progress as well as their own professional development. However, the review lacks explicit reference to the important roles of cultural education in children's early years, specifically its crucial role in the development of children's cultural identities, contextual understanding and dispositions for learning.

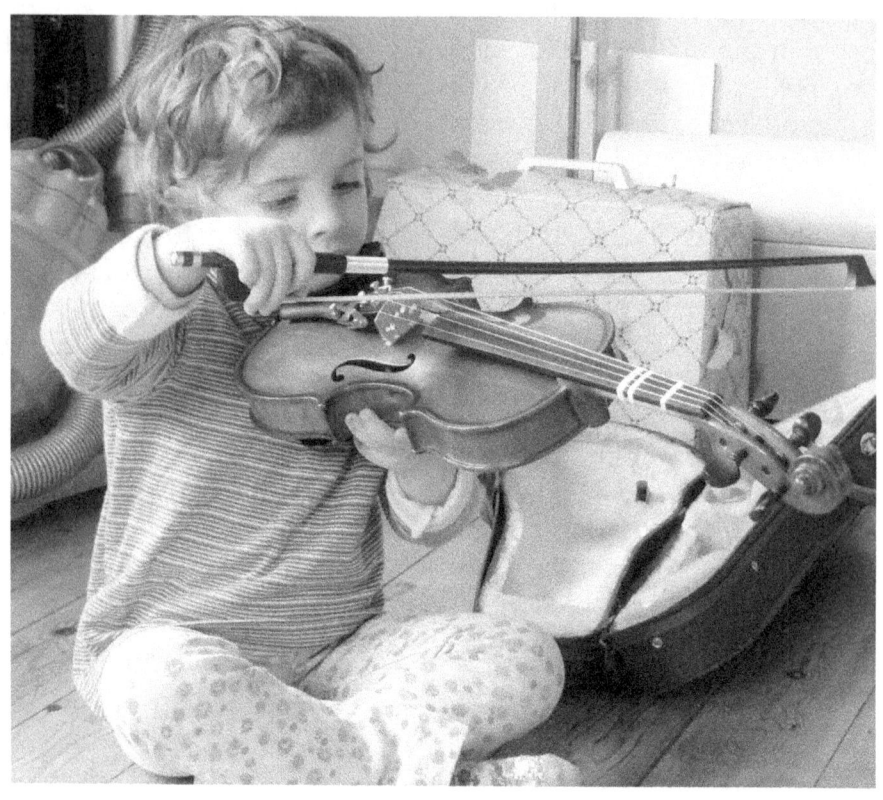

Early Years Confidence in Music initiative. Image by Ruth Churchill Dower

National Initiatives underpinning children's entitlement to culture

- **14 – 19 Creative and Media Diploma** - one of 14 specialised diplomas, providing programmes of learning consisting of different pathways rooted in the needs of the Creative Industries.

- **Arts Awards** - a national qualification which supports young people (17 - 25 yrs) to develop as artists and arts leaders.

- **Artsmark** - a national award scheme recognising schools with a high level and quality of arts provision.

- **C4EO** - The Centre for Excellence and Outcomes in Children and Young People's Services is a dynamic organisation, developed for the children's sector, from the children's sector. C4EO aims to help those working in children's services improve the life chances of all children and young people, in particular those who are most vulnerable. See C4EO's 2011 briefing paper – a short policy context to delivering children's services in the UK and other parts of the world.

- **Campaign for Learning** - promoting family learning at the heart of social inclusion.

- **Children's Commissioner for England** (Maggie Atkinson) - has published findings from its School Exclusions Inquiry in the report, 'They Never Give Up On You''. It finds most schools work hard to cater for troubled students.

- **Council for Learning Outside the Classroom** - programme for arts, culture and creativity outside of formal education.

- **Creative Apprenticeships** - an initiative designed by employers to help companies and institutions train young people in technical and professional skills in the cultural sector.

- **Creative Choices** - gives individuals the ability to find and compare all the courses, jobs, people and placements that are available across the sector.

- **Cultural Olympiad** - Arts Council England's response to the Olympic Games, providing £7m investment including Artists Taking the Lead commissions, capacity building for existing clients, Unlimited – a celebration of arts and disability, 8 Creative Programmers to advise on arts for the Olympics, an International Festival for 2012, and a partnership with the Legacy Trust.

- **Earlyarts** - the award winning, national network for professionals working creatively with young children and families. Provides a range of training, leadership coaching, research and resources for the arts, cultural and early years sector and, importantly, bridges across several sectors enabling them to provide an integrated offer.

- **Engaging Places** - helping schools access inspirational collaborative design, and holistic approaches to the learning environment outside of the classroom.

- **Family and Parenting Institute - Early Learning Partnership Project** - Playing, singing or reading to a young child may seem like an obvious thing to do, but for some parents it is not. The Early Learning Partnership Project is vital for many families across the country.

- **Hear By Right** - tools to help embed the active involvement of children and young people.

- **Inspiring Learning for All** - a self-improvement service for provision across the cultural sector.

- **Legacy Trust** - providing up to £3m for their Creative Legacy for Young People programme, for primary school children to directly participate in creative activities within the context of the London 2012 Olympic and Paralympic Games.

- **Living Places** - a new partnership between the Government and cultural agencies, empowering communities (particularly those experiencing housing-led growth and regeneration) to embed cultural and sporting activity in the development of their villages, towns and cities alongside other key areas of provision.

- **Music Manifesto** – ensuring that all children and young people have access to high quality music education through programmes such as Sing Up, bringing singing to the heart of every primary school child's life, and In Harmony investing £3m in music education in deprived areas, based on El Sistema project, Venezuela.

- **National College** - collaborative leadership programmes for children's services, children's centres and schools, see _Developing Leadership for Creativity in Primary schools_ (2005).

- **National Music Plan** - sets out the central and critical role that music should have in the lives of children and young people. Children from all backgrounds and every part of England should have the opportunity to learn a musical instrument; to make music with others; to learn to sing; and to have the opportunity to progress to the next level of excellence. The plan was initially a recommendation of the Henley Review of Music Education in March 2011.

- **NESTA** - Arts and Innovation research and policy briefing programme.

- **NIACE and Family Learning** - supports parents, grandparents, carers and other family members to be an active part of their children's learning, as well as becoming learners themselves. It includes many different types of activities and takes place in locations as varied as schools, children's centres, museums and libraries.

- **RSA Charter – Education for the 21st Century** - designed to engender a love of learning in young people, and give them the ability and desire to carry on learning throughout life.

- **Specialist Schools and Academies** - helps schools and partners to establish distinctive identities through their chosen specialisms and achieve their targets to raise standards.

- **The Prince's Foundation for Children and the Arts** - an educational charity committed to helping children experience the arts in a high quality and sustained way.

- **The Teaching Agency** - supporting routes into teacher training and professional development.

- **We Think** - explores how the web is changing the world, enabling more people than ever to participate, share and collaborate. It explores culture through democracy, by giving more people a voice, the opportunity to be creative, and allowing knowledge to be set free.

- **Young Enterprise Quickstart Music** - enabling young entrepreneurs to operate their own music businesses with support from music industry mentors.

- **Youth Dance England** - increasing access, raising

standards and improving progression routes.

- **<u>Youth Music</u>** learning and workforce development funding programmes.

- **<u>Youth Sports Trust</u>** - has been instrumental in the success of the sports entitlement initiative, providing both national leadership and local co-ordination.

This is by no means an exhaustive list, and does not reflect the myriad of excellent arts, cultural and creative learning programmes, partnerships, agencies and festivals happening at local and regional levels, many of which can be found on the <u>Earlyarts</u> website.

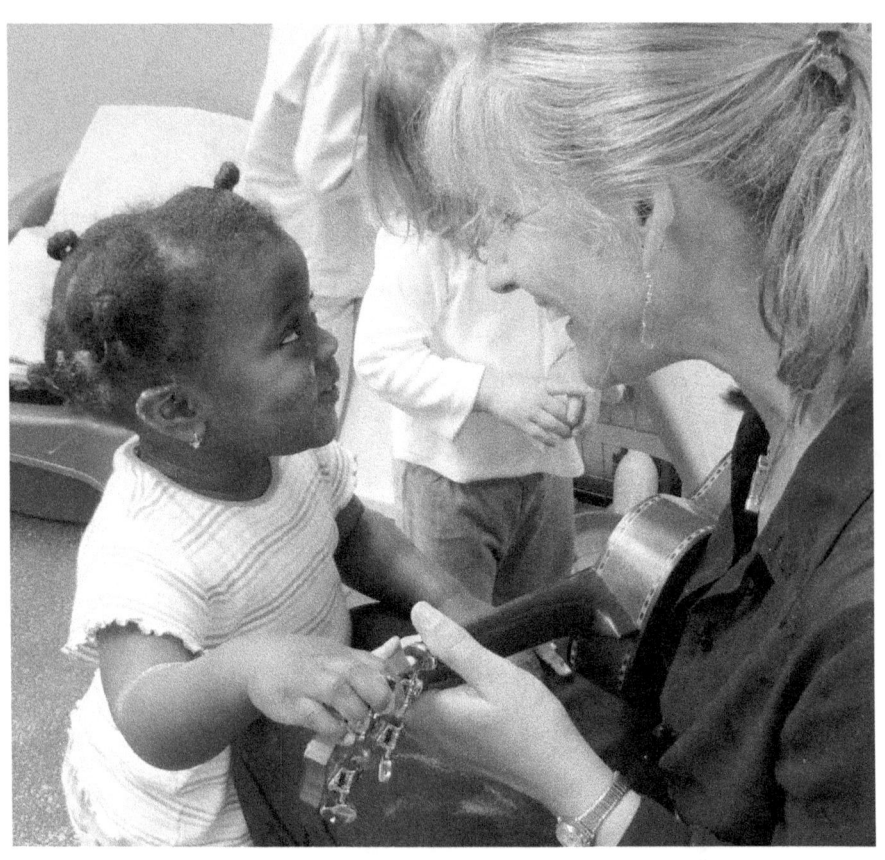

Intergenerational project at a Manchester Family Centre. Image Ruth Churchill Dower

About Earlyarts

Earlyarts is the award winning, national network for people working creatively with children and families in the arts, cultural and early years sectors. Earlyarts members help children have the best start in life by exploring creative approaches to learning, thinking and doing. We help to connect the people, ideas, resources and information that nurture young children's creative and cultural capital.

Join us and start your Earlyarts journey.

Earlyarts' provides:

1. Creative Training – tailored opportunities to build creative skills with Earlyarts partners.

2. Creative Experiences – arts, cultural and creative opportunities for children and families.

3. Leadership Coaching and Masterclasses – exclusive events with experts to help develop strategic visioning, planning and thinking skills.

4. Research and Information – case studies, project ideas, creative research and the latest in policy, publications, curriculum, new initiatives and strategic thinking.

5. Creative Resources – quality products, toolkits and practical resources for creative learning.

6. Consultancy – specialist expertise and knowledge exclusively tailored to your brief.

For more information, see www.earlyarts.co.uk or email susan@earlyarts.co.uk.

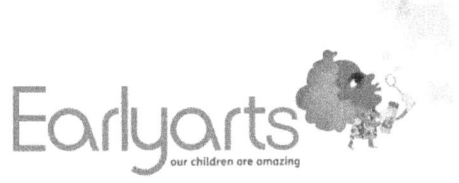

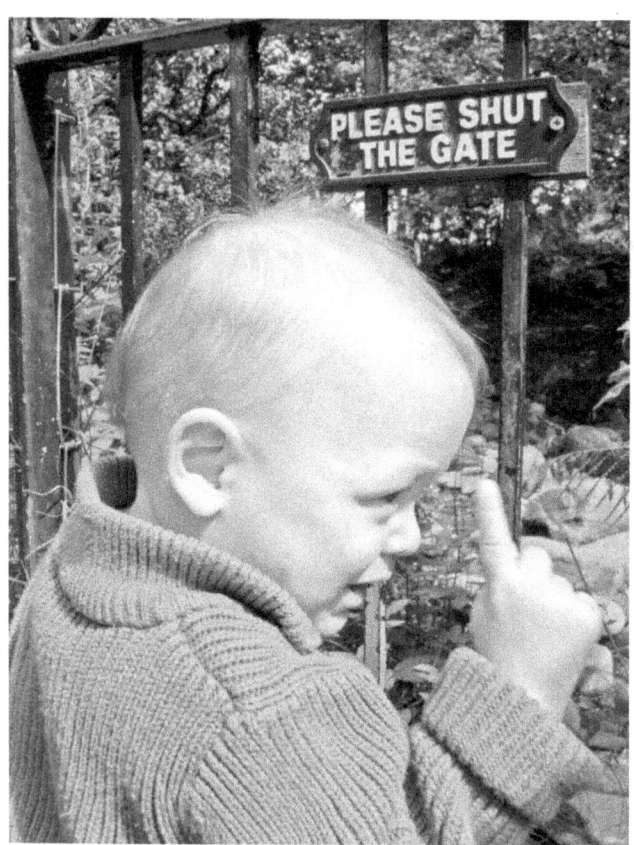

Finding a Voice. Image by Ruth Churchill Dower